Original title:
Laughs Among the Lodgepoles

Copyright © 2025 Creative Arts Management OÜ
All rights reserved.

Author: Robert Ashford
ISBN HARDBACK: 978-1-80567-363-7
ISBN PAPERBACK: 978-1-80567-662-1

A Symphony of Swaying Branches

The trees sway side to side,
Like dancers in a breeze,
Branches twist and dip,
Nature's laughter, soft and free.

A squirrel does a flip,
While birds chirp out a tune,
The sun beams down with glee,
As shadows play and swoon.

Serendipitous Smiles under Starlit Skies

Under a blanket of twinkling light,
Fireflies dance like stars,
Laughter echoes in the night,
As friends share jokes and bars.

A raccoon steals a snack,
With a grin wide and sly,
While owls hoot on the track,
In nature's jest we fly.

Flickers of Fun in Nature's Embrace

Breezes tickle the tall green grass,
As critters scamper near,
Each rustle is a jest,
Bringing joy and cheer.

A wise old toad sits keen,
With stories in his croak,
He knows when to lean,
In the laughter they evoke.

Revelry of the Rustling Needles

The pines whisper secrets in the wind,
As laughter rises high,
With each rustle, a new grin,
Nature's punchline up in the sky.

A jackrabbit hops about,
Chasing shadows in delight,
In the woods, there's no doubt,
Joy is found, day or night.

Hues of Joy Among the Trees

In a realm where shadows dance,
Laughter bubbles, takes a chance.
Squirrels chatter in delight,
While branches sway, oh what a sight.

A bear with shoes, a clumsy feat,
Trips on roots, lands on his seat.
The sunlight filters, golden rays,
Tickling laughter through the maze.

A rabbit hops with silly flair,
Bounding past without a care.
The pine trees nod in gentle glee,
As whispers echo, wild and free.

Breezes carry giggles near,
Nature's stage, no room for fear.
In every nook, pure joy unfolds,
As stories sweetly, softly told.

The Art of Joy in the Grove

Amidst the thicket, chuckles bloom,
With every crack, the echoes loom.
A chipmunk poses for a snap,
While lofty pines create a map.

The fox in shades, a dandy sight,
Donning a bow tie, oh so bright.
While clouds above play peek and hide,
Sunbeams laugh, the world's a ride.

A raccoon jives, a twirl, a spin,
With every step, there's giggling din.
The ground beneath, a stage so grand,
Where critters join a merry band.

With leaves like confetti, they cheer,
Bringing joy, so crystal clear.
In this grove, where whimsy reigns,
The heart of nature's pure refrains.

The Joyful Embrace of Nature

Squirrels dance with glee,
Chasing shadows, wild and free.
A breeze whispers jokes untold,
Nature's secrets, pure and bold.

The sun winks down with glee,
As flowers sway quite playfully.
Clouds are puffs of cotton candy,
While laughter springs, bright and dandy.

A frog croaks out a silly tune,
The raccoons join, a merry croon.
In this realm of green delight,
Every corner sparks a light.

Amidst the trees, joy's a sight,
Where all is silly, sweet, and bright.
With nature's giggles all around,
In every leaf, pure fun is found.

Giggling Leaves

Leaves rustle with a giggly sound,
Whispers of mirth in nature abound.
Branches sway with a playful touch,
In this green world, we laugh so much.

A squirrel slips, what a cheeky blunder,
Catching acorns like lightning thunder.
Each tumble brings a spark of cheer,
The forest echoes, 'Joy is here!'

Dappled light plays tag on the ground,
Chirps and chortles all around.
Every breeze carries tales of fun,
In the laughter of leaves, we run.

The world is painted in silly hues,
With giggling leaves, we chase the blues.
In this playground of trees, folks unite,
With nature's whim, all feels just right.

Revelry in the Pine Needle Carpet

Pine needles plush beneath our feet,
Nature's laughter, a joyful treat.
As we skip through this green parade,
Hearts are light, and worries fade.

The trees wear hats of fluffy snow,
While critters dance, putting on a show.
Every twist of bark brings a grin,
In this wild place, we always win.

The scent of pine, a sweet embrace,
Invites us all to join the race.
Frolicsome times under the sun,
In nature's arms, we have such fun.

Each step is filled with silly schemes,
Chasing shadows, living dreams.
With pine needle carpets underfoot,
We laugh and prance, joy's absolute.

Fables in the Timberland

Timber tales spun by the breeze,
Whimsical whispers dangle from trees.
A raccoon tells of treasures found,
In the laughter of wood, joy is crowned.

Echoes of giggles bounce off the bark,
As fireflies join to dance in the dark.
Fables unwritten, splashed with mirth,
In this woodland realm, we find our worth.

The owls chuckle with sage advice,
While playful winds entice us twice.
Each mischievous creature plays its part,
Filling the woods with love and art.

From silly stories of old and new,
To every glance at nature's view.
In the timberland, our spirits soar,
Where laughter and life forever explore.

Whispers in the Windblown Pines

In the shade where the breezes play,
Squirrels dance in a lively sway,
Branches chuckle, leaves will sway,
Nature's jesters make our day.

Sunlight winks through boughs so high,
While the robins sing and fly,
Frogs croak tunes, a silly cry,
In this woods where giggles lie.

Echoes of Joy between Tall Trees

Underneath the towering wood,
Chirping critters, all in good,
A mockingbird with a punchline's tune,
Leaves rustle like laughter soon.

Beneath the bows where shadows play,
Mice in hats dance the day away,
A chorus of chuckles in sunlit air,
Nature's comedy, beyond compare.

Giggling Shadows of the Forest

In twilight's grip, the shadows grow,
Where giggles echo and soft winds blow,
A rabbit's hop, a playful tease,
The world spins round with joyous ease.

Beneath the moon, a gleeful sight,
Owls hoot jokes in the dead of night,
The forest whispers humorous rhymes,
Bringing smiles through the passing times.

Mirth Beneath the Canopy

Beneath the leaves, a playful cheer,
Acorns fall like nature's beer,
Chipmunks giggle, tails held high,
Under bright and silly sky.

Mossy logs tell tales of fun,
Where laughter dances, never done,
In every corner, joy will bloom,
Beneath the trees, there's always room.

The Mirthful Dance of Sunbeams

In the woods where shadows play,
Sunbeams twirl and glide away.
Tickled leaves begin to sway,
Nature's jests are on display.

Squirrels chatter, jump about,
While butterflies flit in and out.
Every twist and turn, no doubt,
Brings a giggle, quick and sprout.

Little critters, all aglow,
Join the dance, put on a show.
With each turn, the laughter flows,
In the sunlight's golden throes.

Echoes ring through boughs so tall,
Nature's humor, conquering all.
In this mirth, we heed the call,
To join the frolic and enthrall.

Nature's Sweet Serenade

The robins sing with vibrant cheer,
A melody intended here.
Breezes carry joy, my dear,
As nature whispers, soft and clear.

Frogs croak out a quirky tune,
Underneath the glowing moon.
Every thump and splash in June,
Makes the laughter rise up soon.

Dewdrops shimmer on green blades,
As the playful sunlight fades.
A symphony of giggling shades,
Wrapped in nature's thrilling glades.

Laughter dances with the breeze,
Rustling through the swaying trees.
In harmony, they join with ease,
Creating joy, a heart that frees.

The Chuckling Cascade

Water tumbles, swift and bright,
Gurgling jokes, pure delight.
Splashing rocks with all its might,
A circus show, a twinkling sight.

Each droplet plays a trick or tease,
Dancing down with charming breeze.
Nature's laughter, pure as these,
Bringing smiles just like the bees.

Rainbows arch with joyful tunes,
Mischievous as chatty loons.
The cascade hums beneath the moons,
In the night, the laughter swoons.

Joyful echoes, wild and free,
Cascading down, a jubilee.
Among the rocks, a glinting spree,
Nature's mirth flows endlessly.

Amusement in the Shadows

Beneath the trees, the secrets hide,
Whispers giggle, side by side.
Furry friends with eyes so wide,
In quiet nooks, the fun won't bide.

Rustling leaves, a sneaky sound,
Curious critters dart around.
Laughter bounces off the ground,
In every nook, good cheer is found.

Mice in costumes made of grass,
Throw a party as they pass.
Slink and slide, the fun en masse,
Every shadowed crush and clash.

On this stage of bark and bramble,
Nature's jesters prance and ramble.
In the dusk, they laugh and gamble,
As shadows weave a joyful scramble.

The Playful Dance of Light and Leaf

In the breeze the branches sway,
Whispers giggle, colors play.
Sunbeams tickle leaves so bright,
Nature's jesters take to flight.

Squirrels dart with mischief grand,
Chasing shadows, a merry band.
The forest hums a cheerful tune,
Underneath the silver moon.

Chuckles in the Timbered Silence

Beneath the boughs, a secret grin,
Creaking wood as trees begin.
Birds exchange their silly calls,
Echoing through the woodland halls.

Pinecones roll with playful glee,
Woodpeckers drum a song so free.
Rustling leaves, a soft delight,
Laughter dances, day to night.

Frolics under the Rustic Boughs

Rabbits hop in playful race,
Chasing tails, a dappled chase.
Bark and moss, a lively stage,
Nature turns another page.

Chipmunks tease with swift retreats,
Jumps and tumbles, silly feats.
Each rustle reads a story new,
Written by the morning dew.

Snickers Amidst the Woodland Whispers

Wisps of wind in joyful cheer,
Feathered friends come hopping near.
Branches sway with warmth and jest,
Nature's laughter never rests.

Glimmers spark in leafy hue,
Every glance a rendezvous.
As twilight brings the day to close,
A patchwork quilt of joy bestows.

The Spirits of Fun and Folly

In the woods where branches sway,
Squirrels dance and play all day.
A raccoon wears a funny hat,
Chasing shadows, what of that?

Laughing leaves whispering tales,
Of windy pranks and feathered wails.
The brook giggles as it flows,
Sharing secrets only it knows.

Frogs croak jokes, a ribbit spree,
Even the shyest cloud can't flee.
The sun chuckles, bright and bold,
While stories of mischief unfold.

In this realm of playful jest,
The spirits of fun find their rest.
Each twig and stone a partner in cheer,
In this woodland, joy is near.

Tickled by Nature's Breath

Dancing shadows under the trees,
Nature's laughter carried on the breeze.
A deer prances, a hare skips fast,
Whispers of joy in every cast.

Breezes tease the waving grass,
Tickling flowers as they pass.
Bees hum humor in their flight,
While butterflies dance with sheer delight.

The trees sway with a giggle sound,
In the heart of the wild, fun is found.
Even the rocks join in the fun,
With a grin, they bask in the sun.

Underneath the vibrant sky,
Nature chuckles as time flies by.
Each rustling leaf a playful dare,
In this lively world, joy fills the air.

Jolly Tales in the Thicket

Amidst the thicket, stories unfold,
Of critters and antics, brave and bold.
An owl with spectacles, wise yet fun,
Ponders the moon while on the run.

A fox tells tales with a cheeky grin,
While hedgehogs giggle, pokey kin.
Among the ferns, a rabbit box,
Throws a party; come one, come fox!

Chirping birds share secrets of light,
With each flutter, laughter takes flight.
Even the shadows make merry in pairs,
Spinning around in whimsical flares.

Echoes of joy in every nook,
For every heart, a playful hook.
Splashes of laughter ignite the night,
In the thicket where spirits take flight.

The Confluence of Cheer

Where rivers meet in bubbly glee,
Frogs and fish make jokes for free.
A turtle shares his slowest tale,
While dragonflies dart without fail.

The breeze packs puns in every breath,
Tickling whispers of nature's depth.
Joyous echoes of a beaver's laugh,
Build a world of fun on its path.

Dance of shadows, the sun's warm grin,
All around, a marvelous din.
As laughter flows like water bright,
The trees join in with sheer delight.

In this gathering, every heart soars,
The confluence sings of playful roars.
A melody of joy fills the air,
In this realm of cheer, we share.

Lighthearted Tales from the Silvan Heart

In the glade where the critters play,
A squirrel slipped on a twig today.
He twirled and spun in a clumsy dance,
All the others laughed at his chance.

A wise old owl perched high above,
Whispered jokes that the trees all love.
Each chuckle rang through the leaves so bright,
Carried along by the warm moonlight.

Beneath the boughs, a rabbit sneezed,
Sending seeds wafting in the breeze.
The deer snorted, their laughter a cheer,
Echoing joys that all could hear.

With twinkling eyes and frolicsome glee,
Nature's chorus sang joyfully.
Among the roots and the vibrant sprout,
The forest giggles, with no doubt.

Blissful Bonds among the Woodland Giants

Among the giants where shadows play,
Two raccoons put on a mask ballet.
Wobbling about with their crafty flair,
They stumbled and fumbled without a care.

A badger nearby roared with delight,
As acorns fell from the branches light.
Each time they bopped and rolled around,
The merry tunes of laughter were found.

Coyotes joined in with a howl so sweet,
Dancing along on their nimble feet.
With every giggle, the branches swayed,
In the forest where friendships were made.

The sun dipped low, the stars peeked out,
Whispers of joy spread all about.
Nature's secrets in laughter's embrace,
Carried forever in this playful space.

Whispers in the Pines

As the evening fell, a shadow spun,
The pine trees giggled, oh what fun!
A squirrel danced with a pinecone prize,
His little antics brought joy to the skies.

Two owls hooted in a humorous pair,
Trading stories without a care.
The moonlight glinted on their wise, grey heads,
While down below the laughter spreads.

Beetles and bugs joined in the spree,
Creating rhythms beneath the trees.
Each furry creature with a rhyme to share,
In the warm breeze of the woodland air.

As night deepened, the echoes grew,
With every chuckle, the forest knew.
Tales spun softly like a sweet, gentle breeze,
Whispers of joy among the ancient trees.

Shadows of Merriment

In the twilight shade where shadows play,
A clever fox pranced in a bright ballet.
Twisting and turning, a merry surprise,
Made even the crickets all twist to their thighs.

A porcupine chuckled from atop a mound,
Watching the antics all around.
With quills that shimmered like sparkling lights,
Each laugh echoed through the cozy nights.

Hares jumped high in a froggy style,
Creating a scene that would draw a smile.
The air was filled with giggles and cheer,
As shadows danced, the fun felt near.

The stars winked down, twinkling with grace,
At woodland antics and the lively chase.
All creatures united, both great and small,
In this whimsical dance, they had it all.

The Laughter of the Timber

In the shade where branches sway,
Squirrels gossip, come what may.
A raccoon steals a snack with glee,
While spiders spin their webs for free.

The owls chuckle in the night,
As shadows dance in soft moonlight.
Each chipmunk's tale, a grand charade,
Behind each trunk, mischief's made.

Frogs croak jokes upon the log,
Echoing laughter, like a dialogue.
Laughter rings through every bough,
The timber's heart, alive right now.

In the forest, joy ignites,
Nature's stage, with wild delights.
With every rustle, giggles spread,
A symphony of cheer, instead.

Sweet Nothings in the Wilderness

Whispers float through leafy beds,
As critters share their dreamy threads.
A beetle blinks, then takes the floor,
While grasshoppers compete for more.

Beneath the pines, the stories bloom,
Each laughter chased away the gloom.
A clever fox winks with a grin,
His tales of woe are sure to win.

The stream that giggles as it flows,
Knows all the secrets nature knows.
With every splash, each chuckle rings,
Wrapped in the joy that nature brings.

Up high, the hawks exchange their jests,
As wind plays games in the forest nest.
Every nook holds humor bright,
In the wilderness, hearts take flight.

Joyous Revelations at Dusk

As daylight fades behind the hills,
Creatures gather among the thrills.
A bear does a jig, how absurd!
While crickets sing, oh what a word!

The sunset paints the sky in hues,
While busy beavers share their views.
Each twinkling star brings a new tale,
Of midnight pranks, like ghostly mail.

Starlit skies above, so grand,
Shadowy figures take a stand.
The laughter echoes through the trees,
A melody carried with the breeze.

In unity, the voices rise,
With joy unchained, like fireflies.
Each heartbeat mirrored in the night,
As nature revels in delight.

Harmony Amidst the Evergreens

Among the evergreens, a spree,
With whispers carried, wild and free.
A moose prances in his coat,
While penguins plot to build a boat.

The nightingale sings silly tunes,
As bats twirl 'neath the glowing moons.
Each nook and cranny hides a jest,
In nature's play, we find our rest.

Chipmunks chatter, sharing finds,
While shadows dance with playful minds.
The woods alive with every sound,
In harmony, pure joy is found.

With laughter flowing like a stream,
Nature's antics fuel the dream.
Under stars, we laugh and cheer,
In this realm, we shed our fear.

Vibrant Whispers of Merriment

In a grove where shadows dance,
The trees tell tales with every glance.
Swaying branches share their joke,
A knotted root, a playful poke.

Sunlight filters through the green,
Winking leaves in a joyous scene.
Tickled trunks begin to sway,
As laughter rolls through leaf and fray.

Bumbles buzz a silly tune,
While pinecones join the afternoon.
With breezy giggles fresh and light,
The woods are merry, pure delight.

So come and share a lightened heart,
In this realm where fun won't part.
Each rustle, chirp, and flurry of sound,
Holds the mirth of nature unbound.

Whimsical Breezes That Tickle

A breeze tickles the silver leaves,
As nature's jester softly weaves.
The squirrels squabble, a playful chase,
In this woodland, joy's embrace.

Branches sway with laughter bright,
Mice play tag in the soft moonlight.
The owls hoot a silly rhyme,
As echoing giggles sway through time.

Pine needles rustle, secrets shared,
In this place where no one cared.
A frisky fox with a grin so wide,
Darts through shadows, full of pride.

Round and round, the laughter spins,
In every nook where fun begins.
The woods are alive with childish glee,
In every heartbeat, wild and free.

Radiant Smiles at the Forest Edge

At the edge where sunlight gleams,
The mushrooms dance and weave their dreams.
Beneath the boughs, a raucous jest,
Where nature's pranks are at their best.

A rabbit snickers at a hare,
While butterflies swirl in the air.
Each petal flutters, giggles unfold,
A tapestry of laughter bold.

Silly shadows play a game,
A flicker here, a flicker of flame.
The rocks chuckle, a soft reply,
To birds that sing and flit and fly.

So gather round, join in this tale,
Where joy takes flight on every trail.
In vibrant smiles beneath the trees,
This merry world is sure to please.

The Heartbeat of Playful Days

In the heart of woods, so bright and gay,
The sun forms shadows where we play.
A bear dons glasses, looks so grand,
Quite the character in this band.

Chipmunks chatter, fun in their eyes,
As nature's joke unfolds, surprise!
With every rustle, a silly sigh,
The world around us laughs and flies.

Ridding branches of weighty cares,
Every creature shares light flares.
A wise old tree stretches out its limbs,
Holding secrets, laughter swims.

From morning light to dusk's last gleam,
This forest pulses with joy's sweet dream.
So leap and twirl with woodland friends,
In this jolly space, the fun never ends.

Grins Beneath the Evergreen Arc

Underneath the towering trees,
Whispers of joy drift in the breeze.
Branches shake with giggles bright,
As shadows dance in fading light.

Squirrels scamper, tails in flight,
Chasing tales from morn till night.
A sunbeam slides, a prank is played,
The forest's chuckles never fade.

Mossy carpets, soft and green,
The best place for a sneaky scene.
With playful nudges, friends unite,
In the embrace of pure delight.

Laughter echoes, crisp and clear,
Under boughs, their hearts sincere.
Every moment, joy abounds,
In nature's realm, where fun surrounds.

The Cheer of Branching Friendships

Beneath the pines, where shadows play,
Friends gather round at end of day.
With stories spun of silly deeds,
And hearty jokes that meet their needs.

Branches stretch, a canopy wide,
In this wonderland, they confide.
With each chuckle, tales grow tall,
As pinecones rattle, laughter calls.

The creek nearby joins in the cheer,
With bubbly whispers, loud and clear.
Giggling secrets float on by,
Underneath the open sky.

Captured moments, smiles galore,
In every heart, memories soar.
With every hug, they bloom and thrive,
In the warmth where spirits jive.

A Timberland of Sunlit Joy

Raindrops dance on needles green,
In this timberland, joy is seen.
Sunshine peeks through leafy crowns,
Creating laughter, casting frowns.

Wildflowers sway, a playful show,
Bees buzz around with a jaunty flow.
Every rustle, a joke untold,
In this realm, both warm and bold.

Frolicsome breezes weave through the air,
Tickling leaves with a gentle care.
The birds proclaim in chirpy tones,
Echoing laughter in joyful drones.

Adventurous spirits roam the glade,
Creating mischief that never fades.
In this paradise where friendships spark,
Lies a treasure trove of light in the dark.

Secrets Shared in the Sylvan Shadows

Whispers float where shadows loom,
Among the trees, a shared room.
Squirrels peek and scamper near,
In the folds of laughter, all is clear.

Branches arch like open arms,
Welcoming joy, and all its charms.
With cheeky pranks and playful shouts,
In sylvan tales, no room for doubts.

Mushrooms giggle, the ground so soft,
In this hideaway, spirits loft.
Kneeling low, they share a snack,
With wide-eyed wonder, never lack.

Every glance reveals a jest,
In nature's embrace, they find their rest.
Through leafy laughter, bonds are spun,
In sylvan shadows, their hearts are one.

A Chorus of Cheerful Whispers

In the woods, where shadows play,
A squirrel tells jokes in a quirky way.
The breeze carries giggles, light and free,
A symphony of chuckles from every tree.

Branches sway, as the world conspires,
To tickle the leaves with a dance of tires.
Each twig a witness to laughter's charm,
Wrapping the forest in a cozy warm.

Frogs leap about with a croak so bright,
Their antics a sight, what a joyous flight!
While owls roll their eyes at the fuss begun,
In the playful chaos, their wisdom's spun.

So join the frolic, let your spirits soar,
In the forest's embrace, there's joy galore.
With every snicker, the woods are alive,
A hearty chorus makes the wild thrive.

Nectar of Laughter in the Wild

Bumblebees buzz with a ticklish hum,
While flowers giggle, oh, what fun!
Each petal opens with a grin so wide,
As nature's laughter cannot be denied.

Wasps in a tango, a humorous sight,
Dancing on air, they take to flight.
Every leaf rustles with glee untold,
A nectar of mirth, worth more than gold.

In shadows of pines, secrets are spun,
Mice play charades, on the forest run.
Their tiny mischief brings pure delight,
Under the moon's soft and silvery light.

Join in the fun, let your heart be light,
In this wild realm, spirits ignite.
For laughter is shared, and joy's the key,
Come taste the sweetness, wild and free.

The Magic of Forest Jests

Beneath the tall trees, magic unfolds,
With each little creature, a tale that upholds.
Chipmunks make puns, as they scurry and steal,
Sharing their secrets with laughter that's real.

A fox in a cloak of autumn hues,
Slyly steals snacks while the deer snooze.
With every twirl, the leaves seem to wink,
Inviting us closer, to share and to think.

The brook giggles softly as it flows along,
Carrying whispers like a sweet, silly song.
Mushrooms chuckle, with spores that they share,
In this land of mirth, there's joy everywhere.

So wander the trails where the funny resides,
In the heart of the woods, where laughter abides.
Each jest and each grin, like petals in spring,
Woven together, a symphony sings.

Ecstatic Echoes in the Pines

In the depth of the woods, the echoes ring clear,
With every sweet jab, and a chorus of cheer.
Woodpeckers tap out a rhythm of play,
While the sunbeam's laughter brightens the day.

Falcons are jesters, soaring up high,
With each agile dive, they puncture the sky.
Down below, rabbits race in their spheres,
With antics that spark the loudest of cheers.

Pine cones roll over, a game so absurd,
While branches sway gently, unheard, unheard.
The forest, a playground, for creatures all kind,
Where every mischief leaves no one behind.

So dance in the glades, let your worries be light,
Join the woodland memoir, on this joyful flight.
For in every moment, let the laughter entwine,
In the echoes of pines, joy and jest shine.

Caring for the Echoes

In the forest, echoes play,
A cackle lifts and drifts away.
Trees lean in, with knotted smiles,
Sharing giggles across the miles.

The squirrels dance, their tails in flight,
Chirping jokes that feel just right.
Branches sway, a silent cheer,
Nature laughs, and all can hear.

With every rustle, cheer takes wing,
A chorus formed from everything.
The breeze joins in, a playful jest,
In this embrace, we find our rest.

So let us gather, here we'll stay,
Find joy in whispers day by day.
For in these woods, we find our tune,
Echoes bright under the moon.

Whispers of Delight in Wooded Realms

Amidst the trees, secrets unfold,
Soft chuckles in the air, untold.
Leaves dance lightly, a swirling spree,
Tickling hearts, just you and me.

Mocking birds sing silly rhymes,
Toasting to the silliest times.
Mushrooms giggle, green caps high,
As critters gather, oh my, oh my!

Sunlight beams through branches wide,
Shadows play, where joy can hide.
Laughter lingers, playful and sweet,
In snug nooks, where pathways meet.

Woodland tales, wrapped in cheer,
Nature's joy is always near.
In these realms, delight we chase,
Amidst the trees, we find our place.

The Lightness of Being Among Trees

Fluttering leaves whisper sweet,
In this realm, our hearts can meet.
Branches stretch, just like our dreams,
Woven gently in silver streams.

A rabbit's hop, a playful race,
A band of friends in nature's grace.
With every step, we skip and sway,
Finding joy in brightening day.

Up high, the woodpecker taps away,
A lively beat that holds at bay.
Even the shadows seem to grin,
Encouraging laughter to begin.

So let us dance beneath the sky,
In this woodland, spirits fly.
With light hearts, we're free to roam,
Among the trees, we feel like home.

Moments of Merriment in the Forest

Nestled here, where silence sings,
Laughter bubbles, joy it brings.
Mossy seats where friends convene,
Nature's stage, a vibrant scene.

Berries blush, like tickled cheeks,
In this haven, joy peaks.
Breezes play hide-and-seek,
As time drifts in, a gentle streak.

Rustling bushes, critters prance,
Every glance sparks a glance.
Tiny feet tap a merry beat,
In this place, our hearts do meet.

So hold tight these moments here,
Forest fun and every cheer.
Together we weave stories bright,
In the woodland's warm invite.

Smiles Cradled by Bark

Under the trees, shadows play,
Squirrels dance and bounce away.
Leaves rustle softly, secrets shared,
Nature whispers, all is prepared.

Bunny hops with a cheeky flair,
Chasing shadows without a care.
Pinecones roll, a merry race,
Giggles echo in this place.

The sun peeks through, a wink so bright,
Fairies giggle in pure delight.
Branches sway, with laughter's cheer,
A symphony that's crystal clear.

In this grove where joy takes flight,
Friendship blooms, a wondrous sight.
Crisp air filled with fun and glee,
In nature's arms, we're wild and free.

Radiant Giggles at Twilight

As day departs, the stars take stage,
Fireflies twinkle, a glowing page.
Crickets chirp their nightly score,
Whispers of joy forever more.

The breeze carries laughter anew,
A friendly gathering in the dew.
Moonlight dances on eager toes,
Hidden tales where mischief flows.

Hearts unite, in silliness shared,
Under the sky, all burdens bared.
Branches sway with an inviting call,
Magic happens in the fall.

As twilight deepens, we all find,
The warmth of memories intertwined.
In this realm of glowing grace,
Smiles abound in this sacred space.

Frolics in the Evergreen Haven

Among the pines, we take our stand,
Laughter spills like grains of sand.
Playful whispers, echoes bright,
All around, pure delight.

Twirling leaves, a colorful show,
Round and round, we spin and glow.
Joyful antics weave a thread,
Where every giggle is gently fed.

A friendly tug on a favorite hat,
Chasing shadows, then a friendly spat.
The forest floor, a stage so grand,
In this haven, we take our stand.

With every breath, the world ignites,
Laughter glows in the moonlit nights.
Evergreen hugs, a gentle embrace,
In this space, we find our place.

Delights Between the Branches

Beneath the boughs, a raucous cheer,
Stories loom as friends draw near.
Laughter cascades like morning dew,
In this grove, hearts feel brand new.

A squirrel chases a crafty mate,
Twisting vines, it seals its fate.
Jokes unfold behind the bark,
Each turn reveals a playful spark.

The air is thick with chuckles bright,
Every moment turns into light.
In leafy chambers, we all collide,
In joyful moments, side by side.

The night wraps us in a cozy shroud,
We share our dreams, we laugh out loud.
Songs of merriment seem to soar,
In our hearts, forever more.

Sweet Laughter in the Pines

In the shade where shadows play,
Squirrels chase their tails all day.
A chipmunk's dance, a comic sight,
Turns the forest into pure delight.

The breeze carries echoes of cheer,
As branches sway, we gather near.
With every rustle, a giggle grows,
Nature's quirks put on grand shows.

A tumble here, a stumble there,
In this realm, we shed our care.
Pine cones drop, like playful tricks,
We laugh as nature's humor clicks.

Under the boughs, we tell our tales,
Of mischief played by winds that wail.
With every chuckle, hearts take flight,
In the woods, laughter feels so right.

Cherished Giggling Under the Sky

Under skies of azure hue,
We share stories, both old and new.
A rabbit hops, as if on cue,
Chasing laughter like morning dew.

With petals bright, we play and spin,
Each moment soaked in joy within.
A light-hearted breeze brings forth a tune,
While we dance 'neath the glow of the moon.

The sun peeks in, a playful tease,
As shadows stretch like fingers on trees.
A whisper laughed, a secret shared,
In this space, our hearts are bared.

With giggles low and voices high,
We celebrate life beneath the sky.
In this delight, we find our song,
In nature's arms, we all belong.

Treasures of Joy within Nature's Hold

Beneath the trees, where wonders roam,
We find our treasures, far from home.
A flower's giggle, a brook's soft sigh,
Nature's jesters, oh my, oh my!

The rustling leaves play symphony sweet,
Where critters scamper, and mischief can't be beat.
The sunbeams dance on mossy floor,
Each twinkle whispers, 'Come explore!'

A bumblebee buzzes, then takes a leap,
Into blossoms, where secrets sleep.
With every step, adventure unfolds,
In this laughter, life never grows old.

Echoes of joy swirl in the air,
A chorus of happiness, light as a prayer.
In nature's grip, our spirits soar,
Finding treasures that we adore.

Silhouettes of Happiness in the Forest

As twilight drapes a golden hue,
We gather 'round, old friends and new.
The stars peek out, with a wink and grin,
In this embrace, our laughter begins.

Silhouettes dance against the trees,
A waltz of shadows caught in the breeze.
With every chuckle, the night takes flight,
Turning silence into pure delight.

With critters watching, amused and bold,
We share our antics, stories retold.
Underneath the canopy's magic spell,
In every giggle, our hearts dwell.

Whispers of joy like fireflies gleam,
In the night's embrace, life feels like a dream.
In this forest, where happiness glows,
We find the beauty that laughter bestows.

The Sound of Soft Chuckles

In the glade where shadows play,
Whispers tickle the bright bouquet.
Squirrels dance on branches high,
While giggles bounce, oh so spry.

A frog in jest leaps with flair,
As birds join in with songs to share.
The breeze carries a gentle tease,
Nature grins with utmost ease.

Leaves shimmy in a lighthearted way,
As sunlight sprinkles warm ballet.
Every critter holds its breath,
Waiting for the next good jest.

In this realm of playful glee,
Joy bursts forth, wild and free.
With every rustle, laughter flows,
In the woods where humor grows.

Sprightly Spirits in the Forest

Amidst the trunks, a raucous scene,
With sneaky sprites that intervene.
They tickle toes with nimble feet,
And chase the sun, a merry feat.

The owls hoot with a knowing wink,
As squirrels scamper, quick as a blink.
They play hide and seek among the ferns,
Where even the shyest creature learns.

A raccoon juggles acorns galore,
While laughter echoes from woodland's core.
Each creature spins a tale of cheer,
In this lively world where joy is near.

Under the boughs, sweet giggles ring,
In every nook, the forest sings.
Sprightly spirits weave delight,
In the magical embrace of light.

Dancing Shadows of Joy

Beneath the boughs, shadows swirl,
As nimble feet begin to twirl.
The wind carries a playful tune,
While daisies nod, a merry croon.

Pinecones tumble with a thud,
A humorous sound like a soft thud.
Bumblebees buzz with silly zeal,
As laughter tumbles like a wheel.

The brook babbles, a chortling stream,
Where giggling fish jump in a dream.
Every ripple ripples back,
A comical path on nature's track.

In the twilight, the moonlit glow,
Brings laughter where the wild winds blow.
Dancing shadows twist and bend,
In this forest, joy won't end.

Mirth Beneath the Green Canopy

In the shade, where secrets dwell,
Lively tales weave a merry spell.
The critters wink with cheeky pride,
As butterflies flit side by side.

A chipmunk grins, its cheeks all full,
While tree trunks guard this playful jewel.
Whispers flutter like petals in flight,
As chortles blend with the soft twilight.

The branches sway with rhythmic cheer,
Echoing laughter for all to hear.
Each leaf rustles with stories bright,
In the green where joy takes flight.

Mirth blooms beneath the leafy dome,
In every heart, the woods feel like home.
With every giggle and playful glance,
The forest leads the most joyful dance.

Whimsy in the Woodland

In the shade where wildflowers dance,
A squirrel pranks with a silly glance.
The owls hoot in a comical way,
As the sun sets, they too want to play.

With giggles that tumble like leaves in the breeze,
The frogs croak jokes with the greatest of ease.
Even the branches start swaying in glee,
While the rabbits are rolling, wild and free.

A raccoon throws a party at the old oak,
Jokes and laughter, oh what a hoax!
Everyone joins with a little jump and skip,
Nature's own laughter, a humorous trip.

In this woodland realm where whimsy begins,
Every creature knows the fun never ends.
So come take a stroll under skies so fair,
Where merriment dances in the cool, fresh air.

Heartbeats of Happiness in Nature

Butterflies twirl in a polka parade,
While bees buzz sweetly, a joyful serenade.
Mice share tales with a hint of delight,
Under the stars that twinkle so bright.

The brook giggles as it hops over stones,
Tickling the toads with its cheerful tones.
A family of deer plays hide and seek,
With giggles that echo from valley to peak.

Chipmunks in hats, oh what a sight,
They're planning a fest every Friday night.
With acorns as treats, a banquet so grand,
Their laughter spreads across the soft land.

In every rustle, in every small sound,
Happiness thrives, joy knows no bound.
Nature's warm heartbeat gives rise to cheer,
In this haven, delight's always near.

Ecstasy in the Secluded Glade

In a glade where the sunlight beams,
The rabbits plot the most playful schemes.
A chipmunk juggles berries with flair,
Creating a ruckus that fills the air.

The breeze whispers secrets to the tall grass,
While the butterflies flutter, like moments that pass.
With flowers in bowties, they waltz in a line,
In the heart of the woods, everything's fine.

A fox tells stories, a sly, clever prose,
As the thrush cleverly rustles, a way to propose.
The laughter it carries floats high above,
In this tranquil space, there's so much love.

From dusk until dawn, the fun never fades,
As nature's own jesters dance in the shades.
So linger awhile in this joyful spree,
For happiness flourishes where minds can be free.

The Sway of Silvery Firs

Underneath the silvery firs so tall,
Laughter erupts, a most joyful call.
A family of raccoons in mismatched shoes,
Strut like models, all set to amuse.

The breeze carries giggles through branches above,
As squirrels tease chipmunks, oh what a love!
Frogs on their lily pads making a splash,
With a croak and a laugh, it's quite the bash.

As evening sets in, stars twinkle bright,
Nature's own comedy takes flight at night.
The shadows play tricks, they pirouette round,
In a dance of delight, joy truly abounds.

So join in the fun beneath starlit skies,
Where laughter and playful antics gladly arise.
The sway of the silvery firs calls you near,
In this woodland theatre, let's share a cheer!

Lively Jests in the Grove

In the shade where whispers play,
Squirrels dance without delay.
They chase their tails, a comical sight,
While birds gossip from morning till night.

A rabbit hops with a cheeky grin,
Challenging friends to a silly spin.
The sunbeams twinkle with delight,
In this playful world, everything feels right.

Breezes carry laughter sweet,
As toadstools gather for a fun meet.
They tip their caps and jest so grand,
In this secret club where giggles stand.

Every corner hides a playful tease,
Where nature's charm is sure to please.
With every rustle, a vibrant cheer,
In the lively grove, joy is near!

Anecdotes of Joy Beneath the Canopy

Beneath the boughs where stories bloom,
A raccoon snores in a soft costume.
He dreams of snacks both big and small,
While chipmunks stage a wild ball.

Tall trees whisper old silly tales,
Of daring feats and goofy fails.
With each tale spun, a chuckle shared,
In this realm where no one is scared.

A fox in boots struts like a king,
Declaring, 'Watch me do my thing!'
Laughter rings through leafy veins,
Filling hearts and easing pains.

So come gather round, let stories flow,
With each fresh yawn, let spirits grow.
Under the canopy, life's a game,
In this comedy, we're all the same!

A Symphony of Silly Shadows

In a patch where shadows sway,
A turkey gobbles in a bright ballet.
He spins and twirls, quite the sight,
While laughter echoes, hearts feel light.

Mice don tiny hats, strut with flair,
Holding their own show without a care.
The sun dips low, and shadows play,
Creating magic as night meets day.

A snake slides through with a cheeky grin,
Telling secrets where no eyes have been.
Frogs applaud with leaps and croaks,
Sharing the joy in playful jokes.

So sway along with nature's cheer,
Let silly shadows draw you near.
In this symphony, laughter reigns,
Where every note brings light to mundane!

Chuckles Wrapped in Nature's Arms

Crickets chirp a funny song,
Reminding us that laughter's strong.
As daisies sway in gentle grace,
This wild haven is our happy place.

Bees buzz round with gossip sweet,
Sharing secrets of every treat.
While flowers giggle at the bees' fuss,
In this joyous corner, who'd make a fuss?

A puppy leaps through fern and grass,
Chasing shadows as moments pass.
With every bark, he lights the air,
In this fun-filled realm, there's nothing to compare.

So lean back, embrace the charm,
Let chuckles wrap and keep you warm.
In nature's arms, we'll find our glee,
Together here, forever free!

Merriment Amongst the Twisted Trunks

The trees tell tales as they twist and sway,
Squirrels perform acrobatics at play.
Laughter echoes where the shadows dance,
A jolly gathering, a merry chance.

Branches wiggle with ticklish delight,
As critters debate who will take flight.
The moonlight giggles, the stars join in,
Nature's comedy under the skin.

The wind whispers jokes through needles so fine,
Creating a stage for the wild to shine.
Hooting owls and chirping birds,
A symphony of chuckles without any words.

From knobby roots where mischief breeds,
To leafy canopies supplying our needs.
In this forest fun, with friends all around,
Laughter grows louder, a jubilant sound.

Whimsy at Dusk in the Pine-Scented Air

As the sun dips low with a wink in the sky,
The pines share secrets as breezes sigh.
Frogs croak in rhythm, a silly tune,
While fireflies giggle, lighting up soon.

Branches bend low, as if telling a joke,
Each chuckle awakening the gentle oak.
Crickets join in with a raucous cheer,
Under the twilight, all worries disappear.

A dance of shadows, the branches sway,
Playing tag with the glow of the fading day.
Gnarled roots chuckle where nonsense is rife,
Every moment a stanza, alive with life.

In this fragrant haven where joy springs anew,
The laughter of nature feels fresh like the dew.
Whimsy takes flight on the wings of the night,
As we revel in the woodland's pure delight.

Jests in the Gnarled Roots

Among twisted roots, where mischief is spun,
Furry friends gather, their games just begun.
Bunnies wear hats made of leaves and twine,
While turtles play poker, sipping on pine.

Each trunk bears stories of grins and glee,
As acorns roll by, just wild and free.
A raccoon cracks jokes, sly as can be,
With laughter that rings like a sweet melody.

The forest floor's carpet, all mossy and plush,
Holds secrets of giggles in every rush.
Fungi turn faces, with smiles so bright,
In this whimsy-filled world, we dance with delight.

Echoes of laughter in the crisp, cool air,
Remind us of joy, how funny, how rare.
Rooted in friendship, the gnarled trunks sway,
In a delightful embrace at the end of the day.

The Kindred Spirits of Mossy Logs

Upon the mossy logs, where stories unfold,
The spirits of laughter are lively and bold.
With each little bounce, the mushrooms partake,
In jokes whispered softly, a giggling quake.

Amongst the shadows, the critters convene,
Trading their tales, what a wonderful scene!
A troupe of snails slides in quite a line,
While frogs do their best to perform and shine.

A squirrel tosses acorns with playful intent,
While owls hoot softly, with subtle consent.
They gather together, like friends at a feast,
Sharing their laughter, both merry and least.

Beneath a vast sky where the stars dimly glint,
Life's gentle humor leaves all hearts in print.
Those mossy logs cradle each hearty cheer,
In nature's embrace, we hold laughter near.

Humor in the Heart of the Forest

In the shadows where critters play,
A squirrel stands tall, ready to sway.
With acorns in hand, he leaps with glee,
Racing the breeze, oh so carefree.

The woodpecker laughs with each noisy thud,
While the rabbits spin in a soft, green bud.
Branches shake, and the whispers grow,
Nature's jesters put on a show.

The moose trips over a mossy log,
While the frogs croak jokes, their laughter fog.
Even the trees, they sway and bend,
In this forest realm, where giggles blend.

Beneath the stars, the night unfolds,
With crickets chirping tales bold.
In this heartland, smiles ignite,
As woodland jesters dance in the night.

The Revelry of Bark and Beams

Under the canopy, shadows entwine,
A raccoon dons glasses, oh so divine.
With a wiggle and jiggle, he prances around,
Tickling the trees with laughter resound.

The elders whisper tales from the past,
While the pinecones gather, they're having a blast.
A bear in a bowtie joins the spree,
With a shimmy and shake, he's full of glee.

Beneath the moon, the laughter takes flight,
As the owls hoot jokes, lighting the night.
Fungi are laughing with caps held high,
Jumping with joy, they reach for the sky.

In this woodland hall, joy's never shy,
Where each critter's quirk brings a twinkle to the eye.
With every rustle, the merriment grows,
In the heart of the forest, hilarity flows.

Exuberance in the Understory

Down in the thicket, the fun never ends,
A group of young rabbits, they twist and bend.
They play hide and seek 'round bushes so low,
With giggles and hops, they give it a go.

The wildflowers chime in with colors so bright,
Swinging their petals, what a delightful sight!
A porcupine dances, pokes take a chance,
As butterflies flutter, join in the dance.

Under the leaves, the beetles parade,
With tiny top hats, oh, how they've made!
In this lively patch, every creature's a star,
From the smallest of ants to the tallest of spar.

With laughter echoing, the forest sings loud,
In the cozy embrace of the greenery crowd.
Understory merriment, a joyfully spun tale,
As nature conspires, no moment feels stale.

Joyful Serenades of the Woodland

In the dappled sunlight, the songbirds compete,
With tunes so silly, they dance on their feet.
The chattering squirrels join in to sway,
Bouncing through branches, they frolic and play.

A deer takes a bow, all sport and grace,
While fireflies gather, illuminating space.
Each flicker a smile, glowing bright in the dark,
As laughter surrounds in a joyous spark.

The brook bubbles up with a whimsical tune,
While beavers craft boats by the light of the moon.
With each plop and splash, the mirth is alive,
A festival grows, where good spirits thrive.

Under starlit skies, the woodland awakes,
With creatures of whimsy, the laughter cascades.
In this vibrant splash of nature's delight,
Joyful serenades linger deep into night.

Revelations in the Woodlands

In the woods where shadows dance,
The squirrels plot their next advance.
A raccoon, dressed in chef's attire,
Flips pancakes on a campfire pyre.

Beneath the pines, a secret club,
Where chipmunks practice their own grub.
A bear joins in with a gentle roar,
While critters laugh, and spirits soar.

Scattered leaves, like confetti bright,
Dress the ground for a festive night.
Twilight giggles ripple and fade,
As woodland revelries are laid.

With moonlit whispers, they all share,
A game of tag, without a care.
Each branch that rustles brings a cheer,
In the heart of nature, joy is near.

Jolly Secrets in the Shadows

Underneath the canopy high,
Mice tell tales of a pie in the sky.
Owls hoot laughter, wise yet sly,
As fireflies sparkle, buzzing by.

In the thicket, a merry band,
Frogs in coats, a laughing brand.
They practice jigs on lily pads,
With croaks and jumps, they tease the lads.

A fox wears glasses, steals the show,
While badgers plan a grand tableau.
With popcorn kernels scattered wide,
They share their joy, with arms open wide.

Through shadows deep, the giggles rise,
In every nook, a sweet surprise.
The woodland choir sings so bright,
In jolly secrets, pure delight.

Laughter's Flourish in the Pines

Beneath tall trees, the giggles grow,
As acorns fall, they burst with glow.
Squirrels toss them with glee unmatched,
While branches sway, their laughter scratched.

A porcupine spins tales of old,
Of oddball friendships, brave and bold.
With twinkling eyes, the pine cones dance,
Inviting all to join the chance.

The shadows play with silly pranks,
As laughter flows in joyful ranks.
Each rustling leaf tells stories new,
Of woodland frolics, bright and true.

From dusk till dawn, the night unfolds,
With whimsical whispers that never grow cold.
In the pines, where laughter's found,
The heart of the forest spins round and round.

Dappled Joy in the Timber's Heart

In dappled sunlight, stories blend,
Where woodland creatures find a friend.
A beaver crafts with nimble paws,
To build a stage for their applause.

The trees sway gently, stirring fun,
As shadows stretch to welcome sun.
With mushroom caps for party hats,
The woodland folk are merry brats.

A dance-off starts by the old oak,
With twirls and spins, they laugh and choke.
Each buddy joins the lively spree,
In dappled joy, so wild and free.

As evening falls with stars aglow,
They sing and sway, letting joy flow.
In the timber's heart, pure bliss ignites,
With echoes of laughter on starlit nights.

Amusement in the Breath of the Trees

In the woods where giggles grow,
Woodpeckers tap with a lively show.
Squirrels chase tales, twisting with glee,
While shadows dance, wild and free.

Branches creak with a playful tone,
As breezes carry a chuckle's drone.
Sunlight winks through the curtain of leaves,
Tickling the world where mischief weaves.

Whispers of jests flow soft in the air,
Where boughs sway softly, without a care.
Nature's jesters weave tales that tease,
Sharing sweet moments among the trees.

Laughter swirls in a fragrant breeze,
As creatures play hide and seek with ease.
Branches echo a joyful refrain,
In a realm where silliness reigns.

Laughter's Trail through the Timberland

In a forest where giggles bloom bright,
Every path is a playful delight.
The ground squirrels leap, a comical sight,
As shadows dart for a game of flight.

Echoes of mirth stretch far and wide,
Through tall pines where the laughter hides.
A rabbit snickers, a bear shakes its head,
While the sun dips low, lighting up red.

Frolicsome whispers in the cool shade,
A chorus of chuckles serenely played.
The mossy carpet, a stage for the bold,
Tales of old antics in laughter retold.

Amidst the trees in the evening glow,
Nature's jesters put on a show.
With playful jest, the forest thrives,
In this vibrant land where humor survives.

The Jolly Rustle of Leafy Conversations

Leaves join in chatter, a flickering spree,
As branches sway with whimsy and glee.
Breezes carry tales from the heart of the wood,
Echoing laughter, so carefree and good.

From tree to tree, the branches relay,
Stories of joy that dance and sway.
A chipmunk grins in a sunbeam's glow,
Sharing secrets only nature can know.

Swaying trunks hold the mirth of the day,
In every rustle, a jest on display.
With each gust of wind, the woods come alive,
In this merry land where the happy thrive.

From pine to oak, the fun never ends,
As merry whispers bypass the bends.
In the leafy embrace, hilarity sleeps,
Waiting to spring forth in playful leaps.

Harbingers of Joy among Coniferous Giants

Amongst the giants, a ruckus unfolds,
Where laughter is free and the air sparkles gold.
A moose plays the jester, with ears held high,
While the owls chuckle, wings waving goodbye.

Under the spires where the tall trees grow,
Giggling pixies flit to and fro.
The ants tell stories, round in their line,
While pinecone hats are a favorite design.

In the dappled sunlight, mischief brews bright,
As critters unite, ready for flight.
Caterpillars waltz, in a bumbling dance,
Chasing the shadows in a jovial trance.

The canopy chuckles with each gentle sway,
In this merry theater where laughter holds sway.
Amidst the woods, joy in abundance flows,
With coniferous giants, anything goes!

A Tapestry of Joy Beneath the Boughs

Beneath the boughs, where shadows play,
The squirrels dance and chase all day.
A chipmunk slips with a cheeky grin,
While shadows stretch and fun begins.

A robin sings in a raspy tone,
With every note, they claim their throne.
The earthworms wiggle, the ants parade,
Creating laughter in nature's shade.

The pine cones drop with a clumsy plop,
And giggles rise where the branches stop.
The breeze whispers jokes only trees know,
As branches sway with their playful flow.

In this vibrant realm, where joy ignites,
Even the rocks join in and invite.
A tapestry woven with sighs and grins,
Under the watch of the tall tree skins.

The Spirit of Liveliness Among the Pines

When dawn breaks soft, and shadows play,
The pines all crack jokes to start the day.
A rustling leaf sends the laughter round,
As nature's jesters fill the ground.

The playful breeze has a sneaky touch,
Tickling branches that swayed so much.
With every gust, a chuckle flies,
As critters join in with gleeful cries.

A capricious fox with a laugh in tow,
Dances around with a hog's wild show.
While owls roll their eyes at the little scene,
In this forest stage, the laughter's keen.

Every step brings a giggle, a cheer,
Where pine trees sway, all worries disappear.
The spirit of joy, with a wink and a grin,
Turns solitude's edge into laughter within.

The Forest's Grinning Heart

In the heart of the woods, where the sunbeams dart,
Nature chuckles with an open heart.
A bear stumbles trying to catch a bee,
While the rabbits wiggle with glee—a spree!

The brook babbles jokes to the pebbles below,
Each splash a punchline in the rivers' flow.
A snail on a leaf boasts the speed it keeps,
While frogs leap around, scoring laughter in heaps.

Mushrooms giggle, dressed in their caps,
A merry convention of woodland chaps.
Their vibrant hues echo laughter's spark,
Unraveling jokes in the whispering dark.

The trees they sway, calling all to share,
With breezy remarks flowing through the air.
In the heart of the forest, where joy is an art,
Each creature embodies the forest's grinning heart.

The Delicacy of Humor in the Wilderness

Within the wild, a secret thrives,
Where the laughter of nature truly arrives.
A hawk swoops low with a silly dive,
While ladybugs buzz, adding to the jive.

The sunbeams tickle the mossy ground,
As shadows pirouette with soft sounds.
A playful deer leaps amidst the trees,
The wind carries whispers, tickling the leaves.

Beneath the layers of bramble and vine,
A chipmunk cracks jokes about nature's design.
Even the flowers join in the fun,
With petals that dance, kissed by the sun.

The delicacy of humor, a delicate art,
Where nature's performers play their part.
In every rustle, a story unfolds,
In the wild laughter, adventure beholds.

Echoes Between the Trees

Whispers weave through leafy crowns,
Echoing giggles, nature's sounds.
Squirrels dance with acorn hats,
Chasing shadows, where humor chats.

Branches sway like jolly mates,
Tickling trunks with playful traits.
A rabbit hops on hidden trails,
In this forest, joy prevails.

Mossy carpets, green and bright,
Underfoot, a soft delight.
Beneath the sun, the laughter glows,
Rustling leaves, where cheerfulness flows.

Rusty nails on a wooden swing,
Echoes of joy, let laughter ring.
Nature's jesters in a playful game,
Every corner, never the same.

The Playful Breeze

A gust that tickles through the pines,
Spreading cheer as it entwines.
With every swish, it plays a tune,
Dancing shadows beneath the moon.

Branches bow with ticklish grace,
The wind's a jester in this place.
Rustling leaves in a merry mess,
Bringing smiles, a joyous dress.

Floating whispers, breezy glee,
Nature's laughter, wild and free.
A playful breeze spins tales anew,
Of silly moments shared by two.

With every chill against the cheek,
Laughter echoes, vibrant, sleek.
Banana peels on forest floors,
Tickling toes, as humor soars.

Secrets of the Wooded Grove

Beneath the trees with crowns so wide,
Lies a secret, joy inside.
Mushrooms giggle in the shade,
Winking at the games we've played.

Bushes rustle, what's the fuss?
A band of critters makes a bus!
With tiny hats and sunny smiles,
They journey on, across the miles.

Whispers shared with every breeze,
Jokes exchanged among the leaves.
Hidden paths and trails of glee,
This grove's alive with hilarity.

Bending grass that plays the fool,
Nature's website, the funniest school.
Every nook holds a cheeky tale,
In this green realm, laughter prevails.

Jests Underneath the Canopy

Beneath the boughs, the stories bloom,
In shadows deep, there's always room.
A raccoon's hat, a squirrel's song,
In this place, you'll never be wrong.

Branches sway with silly jig,
Laughter hides in every twig.
A dancing leaf, a bootless bear,
Whiskers twitch, that's quite the scare!

Moonlit nights spark friendly pranks,
Each tree bears stories, laughs in ranks.
With every rustle, joy's decree,
Life underneath, pure jubilee.

Bubbly giggles fill the air,
With every twist, find laughter rare.
In the canopy, let humor thrive,
A forest joke, to keep alive.

www.ingramcontent.com/pod-product-compliance
Lightning Source LLC
Chambersburg PA
CBHW051637160426
43209CB00004B/682